A Prickle of Porcupines / Una manada de puercoespines

By Lincoln James   Traducción al español: Eduardo Alamán

Gareth Stevens
Publishing

Please visit our website, www.garethstevens.com. For a free color catalog of all our high-quality books, call toll free 1-800-542-2595 or fax 1-877-542-2596.

Publisher Cataloging Data

James, Lincoln
[A prickle of porcupines. Spanish & English]
     A prickle of porcupines = Una manada de puercoespines / by Lincoln James ; traducción al español, Eduardo Alamán.
        p.   cm. – (Animal groups = Grupos de animales)
     Includes bibliographical references and index.
     Summary: This book describes the physical characteristics, behavior, habitat, and group life of porcupines.
     Contents: Get the point! = ¡Al punto! – Old and new = Viejos y nuevos – Life in the trees = Vida en los árboles – Ouch! = ¡Uy! – Let's get together = Todos juntos – Baby porcupines = Bebés puercoespín – Time to go = Hora de irse.
     ISBN 978-1-4339-8812-7
     1. Porcupines—Juvenile literature   2. Societal behavior in animals—Juvenile literature   3. Animal societies—Juvenile literature   [1. Porcupines   2. Societal behavior in animals   3. Spanish language materials—Bilingual]   I. Title
II. Title: Manada de puercoespines
        2013
    599.35/97—dc23

First Edition

Published in 2013 by
Gareth Stevens Publishing
111 East 14th Street, Suite 349
New York, NY 10003

Designer: Sarah Liddell
Editor: Greg Roza

Printed in the United States of America

CPSIA compliance information: Batch #CW13GS: For further information contact Gareth Stevens, New York, New York at 1-800-542-2595.

Contents

Contenido

Get the Point!

Porcupines are large **rodents**. All porcupines have a special way of staying safe. They're covered with sharp **spines** called quills. A group of porcupines is called a prickle. A prickle is also a small, sharp point.

- -

¡Al punto!

Los puercoespines son **roedores** grandes. Todos los puercoespines tienen una forma muy especial de protegerse. Los puercoespines están cubiertos de espinas llamadas **púas**. Un grupo de puercoespines se llama manada.

Old and New

There are two main kinds of porcupines. Those that live in Europe, Africa, and Asia are called Old World porcupines. Those that live in the Americas are called New World porcupines. This book is mainly about New World porcupines.

- -

Viejos y nuevos

Existen dos clases de puercoespines. Aquellos que viven en Europa, África y Asia se les llama puercoespines del viejo mundo. A aquellos que viven en el continente americano se conocen como puercoespines del nuevo mundo. Este libro es, principalmente, acerca de los puercoespines del nuevo mundo.

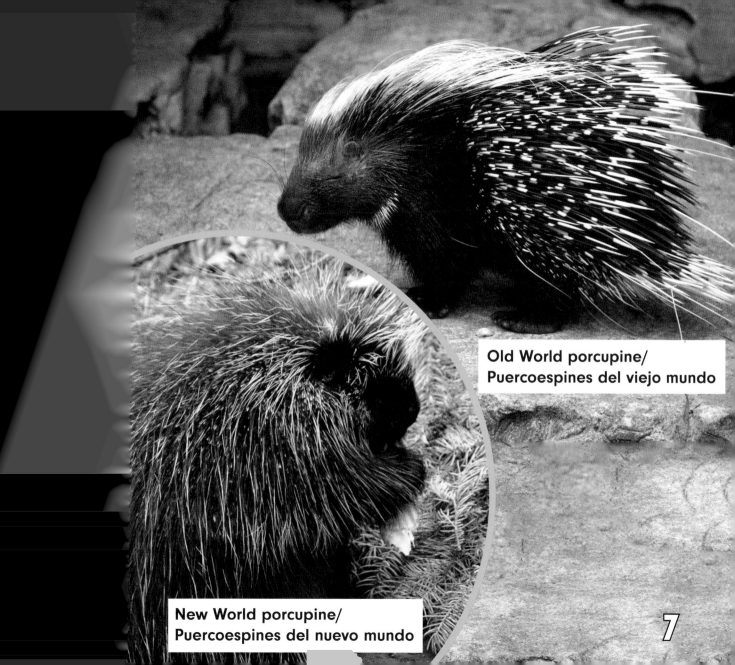

Old World porcupine/
Puercoespines del viejo mundo

New World porcupine/
Puercoespines del nuevo mundo

7

Life in the Trees

Many porcupines sleep in trees during the day. Some sleep in old logs or **burrows**. They come out at night to find food. Porcupines are plant eaters. In winter, they often eat the soft wood beneath tree bark. This can kill the trees.

- -

Vida en los árboles

Muchos puercoespines duermen en árboles durante el día. Algunos duermen en troncos viejos o en **madrigueras**. Por la noche salen a comer. Los puercoespines comen plantas. En el invierno suelen comer la madera blanda bajo la corteza de los árboles. Esto puede matar al árbol.

Ouch!

A porcupine quill is made up of long hairs that have grown together. The quills are usually a lighter color than the animals' fur. This makes them easier to see and tells other animals to stay far away.

- -

¡Uy!

Las púas de los puercoespines están formadas por cabellos largos que han crecido juntos. Las púas suelen ser de un color más claro que el pelaje del animal. Esto hace que sean fáciles de ver y mantiene a otros animales a la distancia.

11

When an enemy is near, a porcupine stomps it feet and shakes its quills. This says, "Stay back!" The porcupine may hit the enemy with its tail. The porcupine's quills stick in the enemy and cause a lot of pain.

Cuando un animal se acerca, el puercoespín azota sus pies y mueve sus púas. Con esto dice: "¡No te acerques!". El puercoespín puede golpear al enemigo con la cola. Las púas del puercoespín se entierran en el enemigo y causar mucho dolor.

13

Let's Get Together

Porcupines form prickles when searching for food. They also share a den during the cold winter months. The largest prickles often have no more than 12 porcupines. Old World porcupines form family prickles more often than New World porcupines.

Todos juntos

Los puercoespines buscan comida en grupos. Además comparten su guarida durante los meses fríos del invierno. Las manadas más grandes no tienen más de 12 puercoespines. Los puercoespines del viejo mundo forman manadas con mayor frecuencia que los del nuevo mundo.

Males and females each have their own **territory**. A porcupine doesn't like other porcupines in its territory. Males and females get together once a year to **mate**. Females often have a single baby. Males don't help raise young porcupines.

Los machos y las hembras tienen su propio **territorio**. A los puercoespines no les gusta que otros puercoespines entren a su territorio. Los machos y las hembras se reúnen una vez al año para **reproducirse**. Las hembras suelen tener un solo bebé. Los machos no crían a los jóvenes puercoespines.

17

Baby Porcupines

Baby porcupines are born in early summer. Mothers raise young porcupines for about 4 months. During the day, the mother sleeps in a tree while the baby hides in a burrow. After about 6 weeks, the mother teaches her baby to find food.

- -

Bebés puercoespín

Los bebés puercoespín nacen al inicio del verano. Las mamás los cuidan durante unos cuatro meses. Durante el día, las mamás duermen en un árbol mientras los bebés se esconden en la guarida. Después de unas seis semanas las mamás les enseñan a sus crías a buscar comida.

Time to Go

As baby porcupines grow older, they spend less time with their mother. In early fall, the female is ready to mate again. The young porcupine wanders off. It may spend the winter alone, or it may find a prickle to hang out with.

Hora de irse

Al crecer, los bebés puercoespines pasan menos tiempo con sus mamás. En el otoño, los puercoespines comienzan a explorar. Algunos pasan solos el invierno o encuentran otra manada.

Fun Facts About Porcupines/ Datos sobre los puercoespines

A porcupine can have up to 30,000 quills on its body.

Un puercoespín puede tener hasta 30,000 púas en su cuerpo.

Porcupines can grow up to 48 inches (122 cm) long, from nose to tail.

Pueden crecer hasta 48 pulgadas (122 cm) de largo, de la nariz a la cola.

The porcupine's sharp claws make it an excellent climber. Some climb as high as 60 feet (18 m) to reach food.

Las garras de los puercoespines son muy filosas y son buena para trepar. Algunos trepan hasta 60 pies (18 m) para alcanzar su comida.

Porcupines are good swimmers! Their hollow quills help them float.

¡Los puercoespines son buenos nadadores! Sus púas huecas les ayudan a flotar.

Glossary

burrow: a hole made by an animal in which it lives or hides

mate: to come together to make babies

rodent: a small, furry animal with large front teeth, such as a mouse or rat

spine: a long, sharp body part

territory: an area of land that an animal considers to be its own and will fight to control

- -

Glosario

madriguera (la): un hoyo en el que vive o se esconde un animal

reproducirse: juntarse para hacer bebés

roedor (el): un animal peludo y pequeño con grandes dientes, como una rata o ratón

púas (las): partes largas y puntiagudas del cuerpo

territorio (el): área que un animal considera como suya

For More Information/
Para más información

Books

Antill, Sara. *Porcupines.* New York, NY: Windmill Books, 2011.

Green, Emily K. *Porcupines.* Minneapolis, MN: Bellwether Media, 2011.

Websites

Mammals: Porcupine

www.sandiegozoo.org/animalbytes/t-porcupine.html
Read more about New World porcupines, and learn how they are different from Old World porcupines.

North American Porcupine

www.nhptv.org/natureworks/porcupine.htm
Read about the North American porcupine, which is the largest of the New World porcupines, and see pictures of it.

Porcupines

www.awf.org/content/wildlife/detail/porcupine
Learn about the crested porcupine, which is the largest rodent in Africa.

Index

Índice